ISBN:

978-1-947215-42-9

Copyright:

TX0008935990

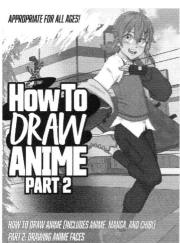

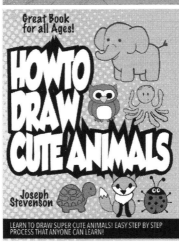

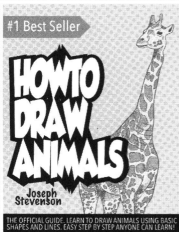

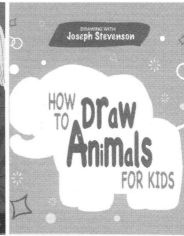

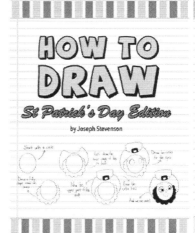

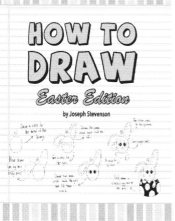

INTRO

It's time to learn to draw Halloween characters! Halloween is actually my birthday and my favorite holiday.

In this and my other holiday themed books you'll find lessons on drawing all of your favorite holiday characters.

I started making these how to draw books because I wanted to help kids learn to love drawing just as much as I do. If you have any questions you can always reach out to me on my website at:

www.josephstevenson.com

In this book each drawing lesson is on it's own page along with a section for drawing yourself. I would love to see what you come up with! Please send me your own drawings on my website and I'll post them in my blog and on social media!

~ Joseph Stevenson

BAT

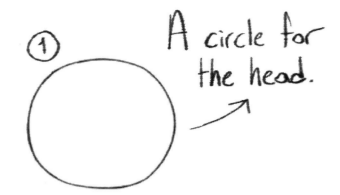

① A circle for the head.

② Two rounded triangles for the ears.

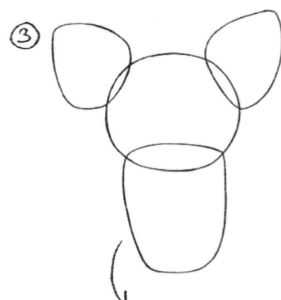

③ A square for the body.

④ Two lines for each leg and draw three sticks for the fingers.

⑤ Erase the extra lines.

⑥ A heart shape for the nose and complete drawing with the details.

SPIDER WEB

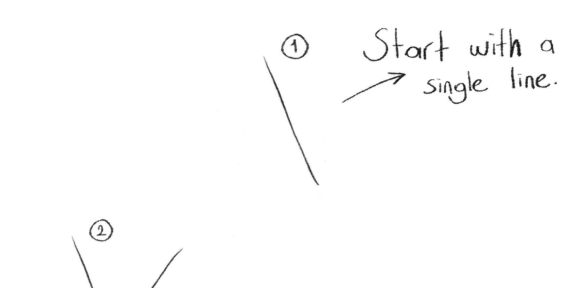

① Start with a single line.

② Draw five more lines.

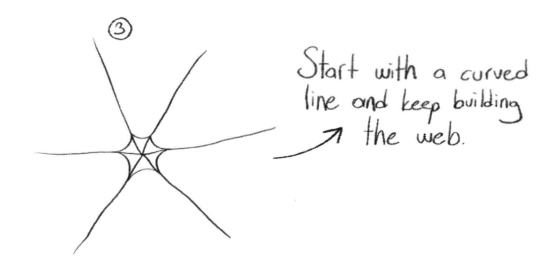

③ Start with a curved line and keep building the web.

④

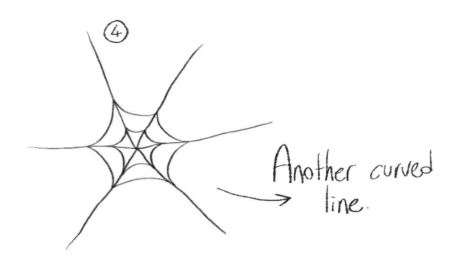

Another curved
line.

⑤

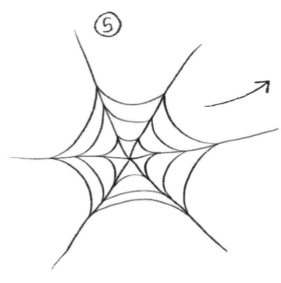

Keep going!

You can add more
lines or stop. It's your
decision!

⑥

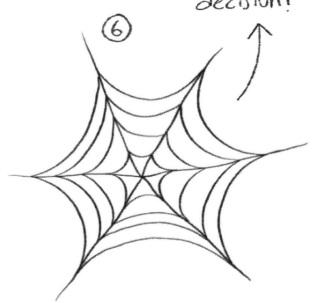

MONSTER

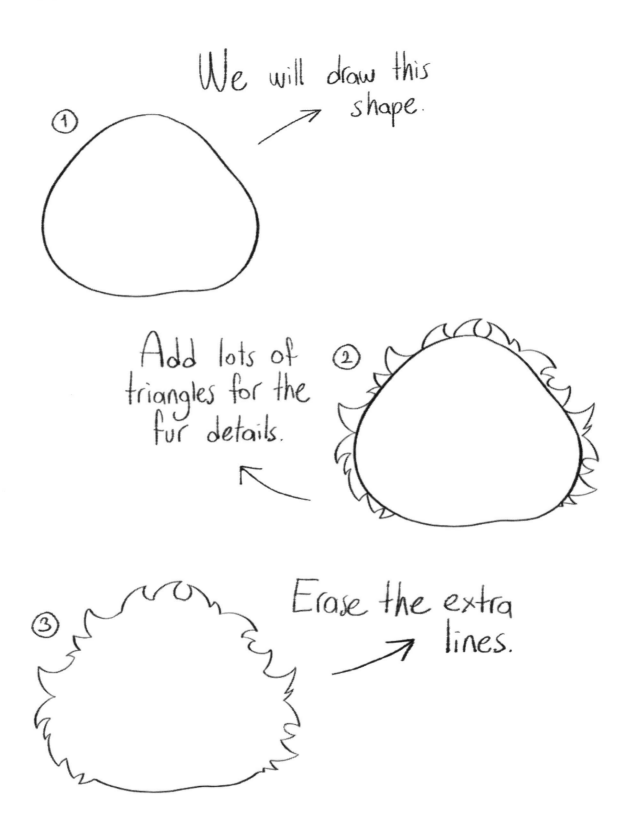

① We will draw this shape.

② Add lots of triangles for the fur details.

③ Erase the extra lines.

A circle for the
eye and a bean
for the mouth.

④

⑤

Another circle inside
the eye and fill it
black.

Teeth and
tongue.

⑥

Add the remaining
lines and we are done!

POTION

A circle for the base
of the bottle.

①

A rectangle on top.

②

Lets add an ellipse.

③

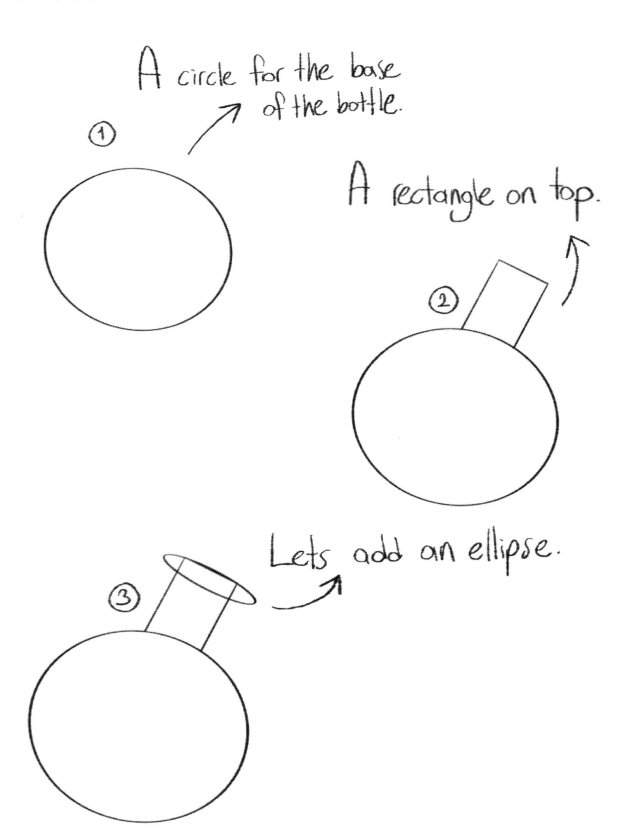

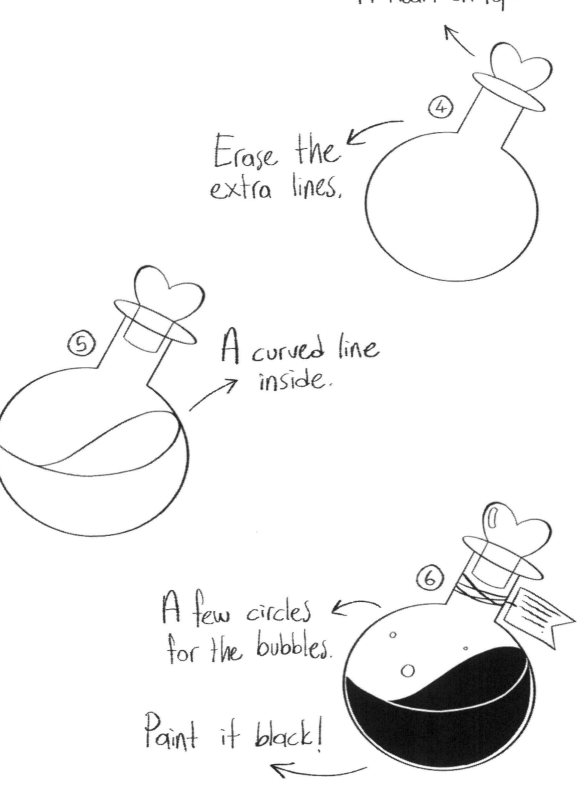

A heart on top.

④ Erase the extra lines.

⑤ A curved line inside.

⑥ A few circles for the bubbles.

Paint it black!

CAULDRON

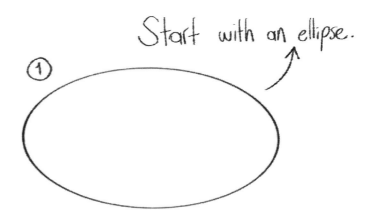

Start with an ellipse.

①

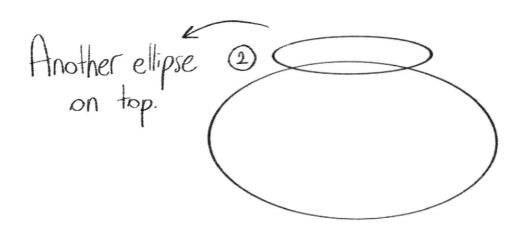

Another ellipse on top.

②

Connect those two ellipses and erase the extra lines.

③

④ Two curved lines for each handle.

⑤ Add this shape.

Three circles for the bubbles.

⑥

WITCH HAT

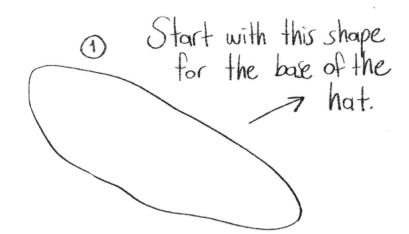

① Start with this shape for the base of the hat.

A not so perfect triangle on top!

②

③ Another triangle but make it thinner.

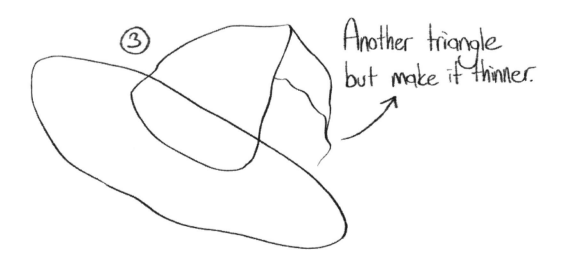

Erase the extra
lines and cut a triangle
from the base of
the hat.

④

Some lines for
the details.

⑤

Draw a big square
and a small rectangle
on top.

⑥

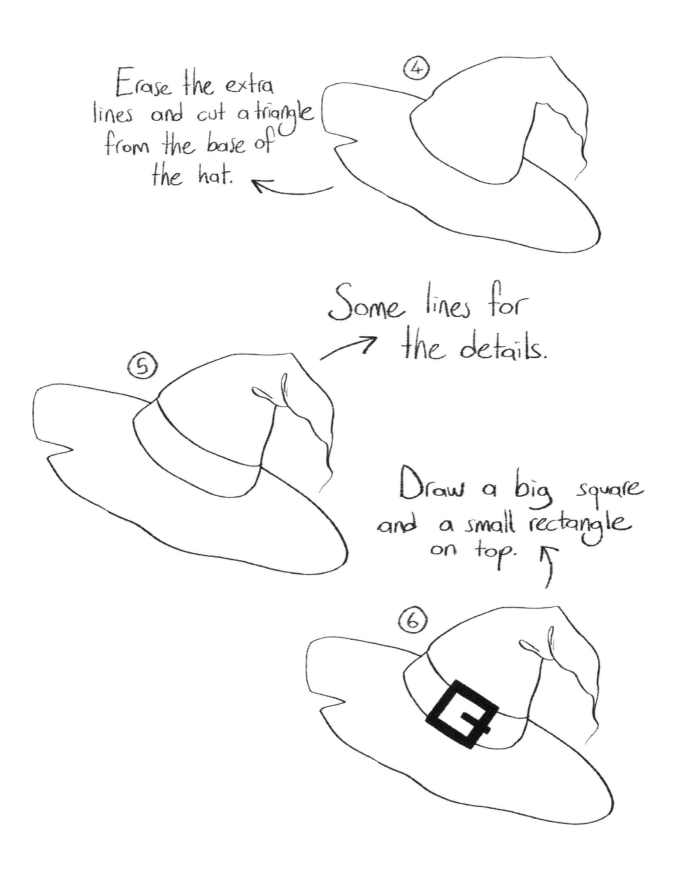

BROOM

Think this shape
a rounded triangle.

①

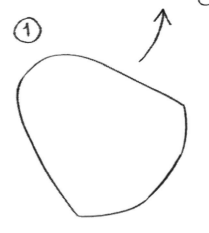

②

Another triangle
but reversed.

Draw a wooden
stick.

③

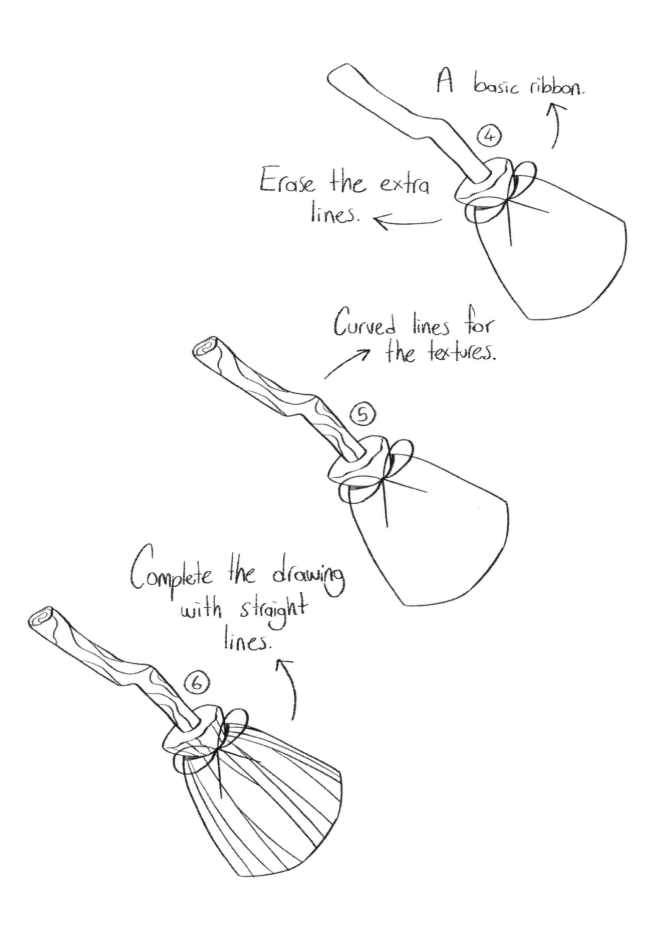

A basic ribbon.

④

Erase the extra lines. ←

Curved lines for the textures.

⑤

Complete the drawing with straight lines.

⑥

VAMPIRE

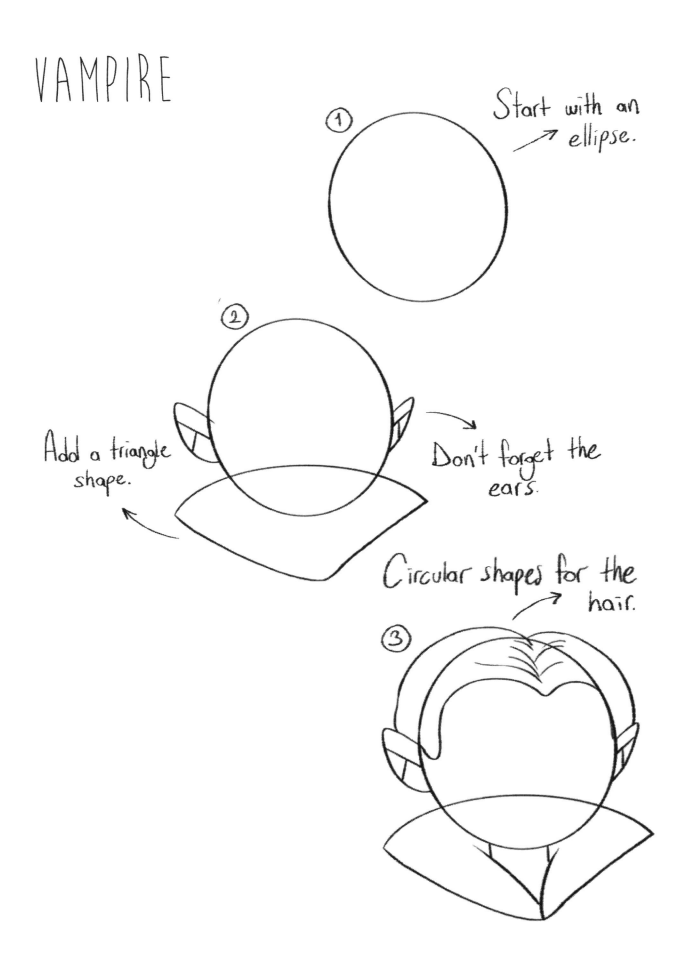

① Start with an ellipse.

② Add a triangle shape.

Don't forget the ears.

③ Circular shapes for the hair.

Some random lines for the hair.

④

Erase the extra lines.

⑤

A triangle for the nose.

Two circles for the earrings.

⑥

Add the remaining details and we are done!

FRANKENSTEIN

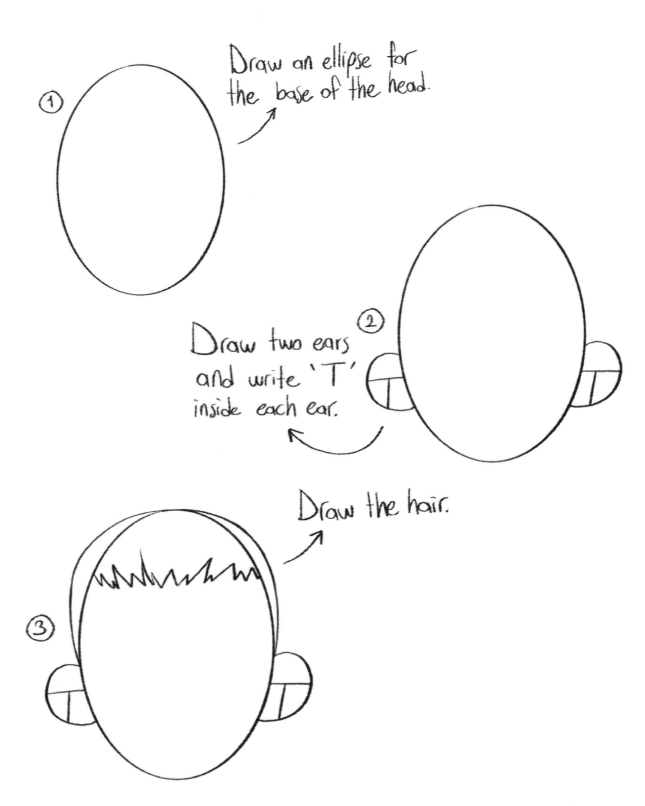

1 — Draw an ellipse for the base of the head.

2 — Draw two ears and write 'T' inside each ear.

Draw the hair.

3

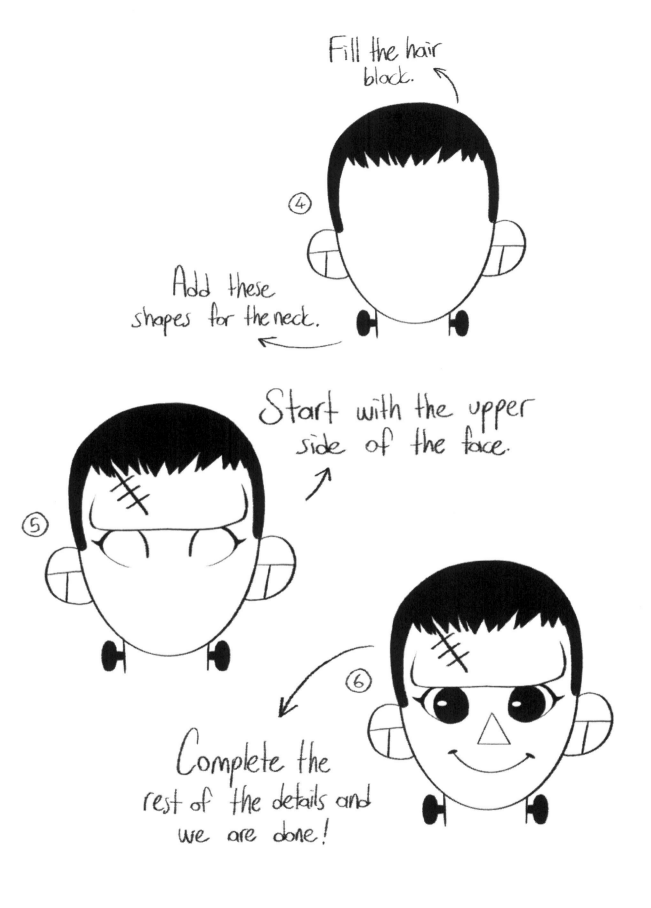

Fill the hair block.

④

Add these shapes for the neck.

Start with the upper side of the face.

⑤

⑥

Complete the rest of the details and we are done!

BAT

① We will start drawing with this shape.

② Two rounded triangles for the ears.

③

Add a fluffy shape.

Add a curved
line inside each ear.

④

Two circular shapes
for the eyes and a
rounded triangle for
the nose.

⑤

Random lines
inside.

⑥

Complete the
drawing with the remaining
details.

BLACK CAT

Start with a circle.

①

Draw two rounded triangles.

②

A rounded rectangle.

A fluffy tail.

③

Think these shapes as rounded rectangles too.

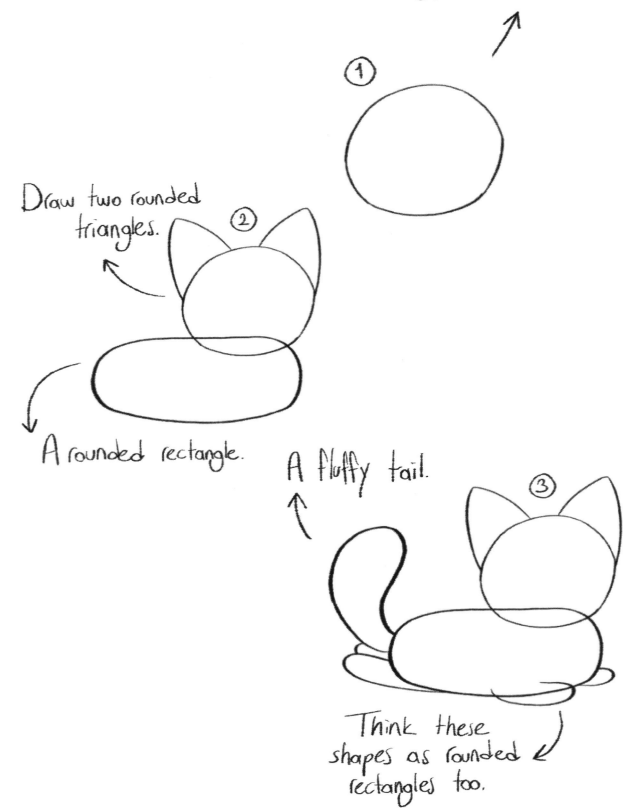

④ Two eyes and a nose.

Fill it black.

⑤

Add the remaining details and we are done!

⑥

OWL

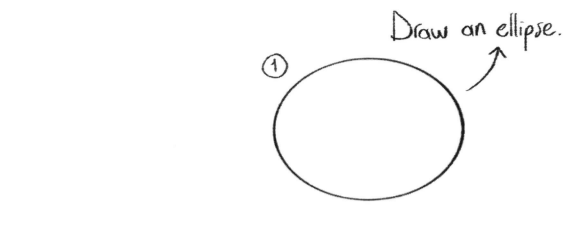

① Draw an ellipse.

② Two triangles for the ears.

Draw two curved lines inside the face.

③ Two circles for the eyes and a triangle for the nose.

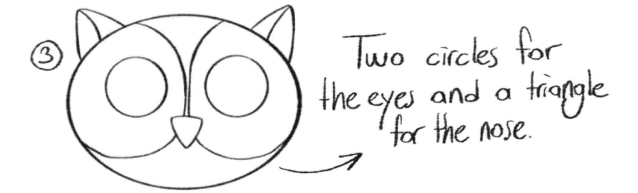

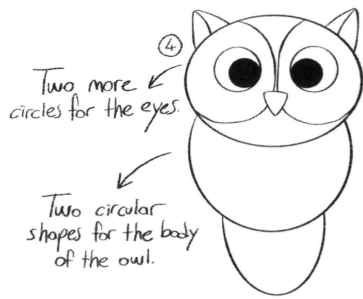

④ Two more circles for the eyes.

Two circular shapes for the body of the owl.

⑤ Don't forget her wings.

Lets complete the drawing with a branch.

⑥ Erase two circles for the sparkle.

MUMMY

Start with these shapes.

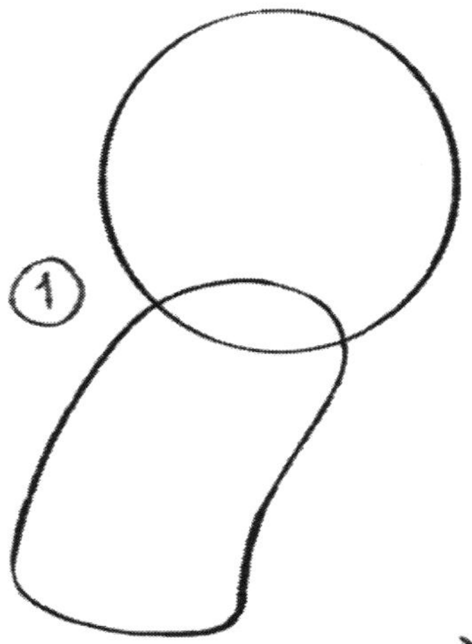

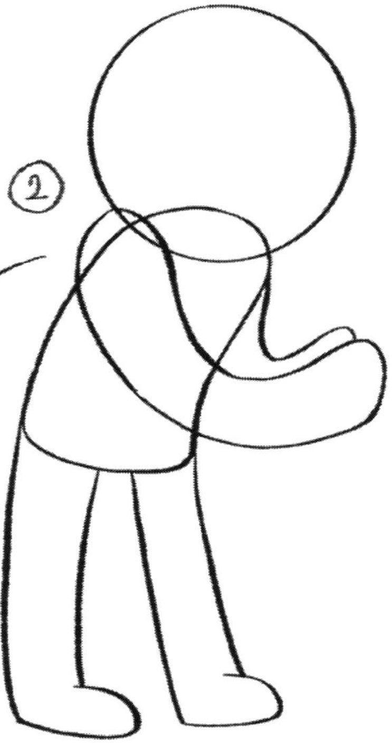

①

Draw the arms and the legs.

②

③

Erase the extra lines.

We will start with the
head and keep building through
the body.

④

⑤

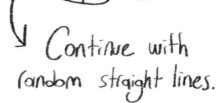

Continue with
random straight lines.

Draw two circle
for the eyes and two
ellipse for the nose.

⑥

PUMPKIN

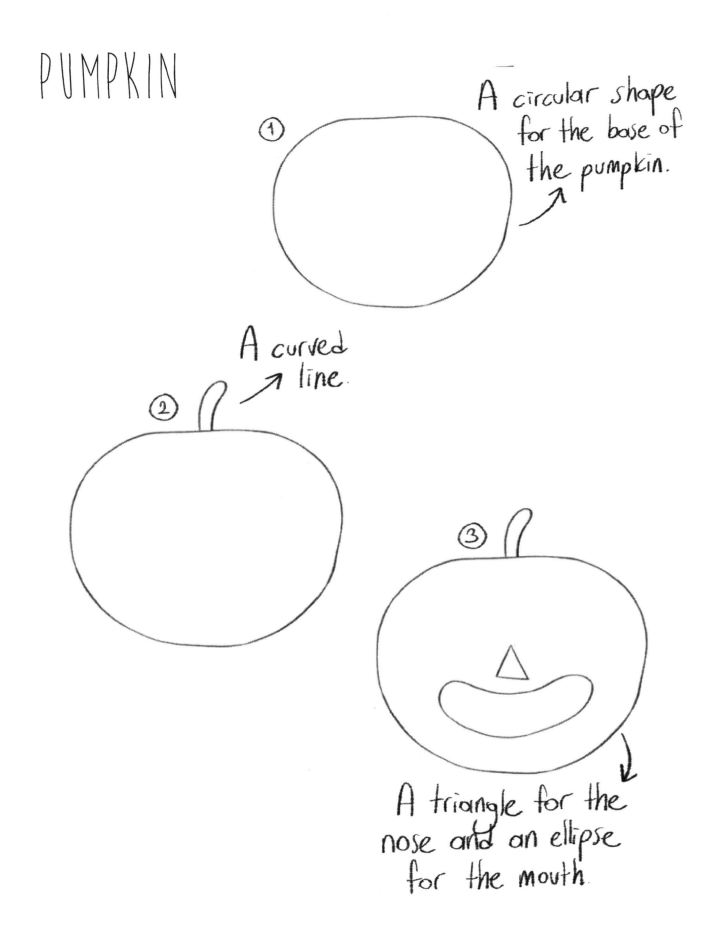

① A circular shape for the base of the pumpkin.

② A curved line.

③ A triangle for the nose and an ellipse for the mouth.

Two circles for the eyes and draw the teeth.

Paint them black.

Draw random straight lines through the pumpkin and we are done.

CANDY

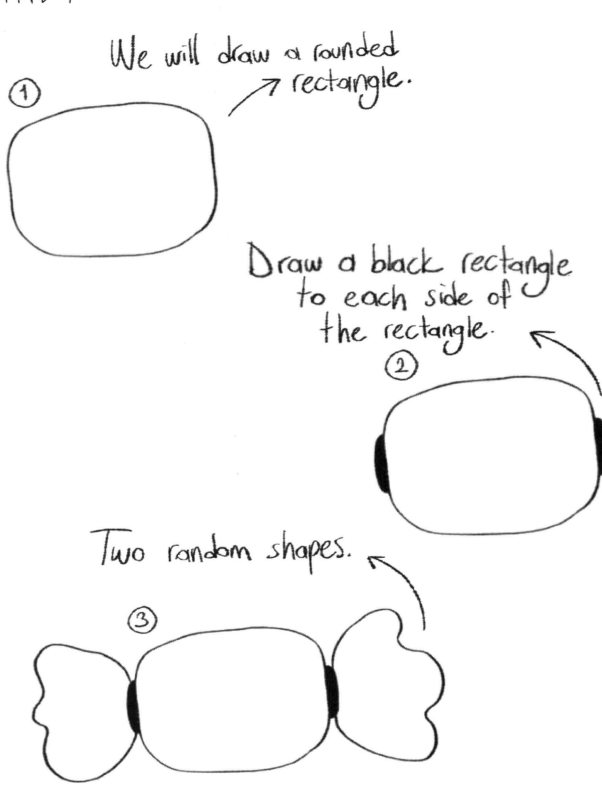

We will draw a rounded rectangle.

①

Draw a black rectangle to each side of the rectangle.

②

Two random shapes.

③

Draw random
lines inside each shape.

④

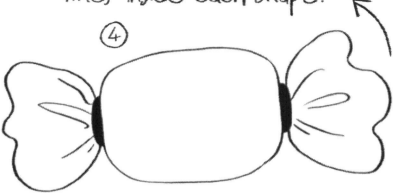

Start with random circles
and fill them black.

⑤

Continue with small
black circles.

⑥

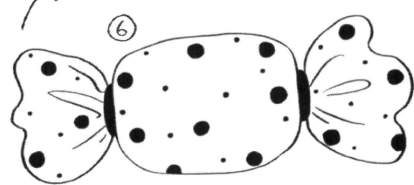

SCARECROW

A circle for the head and a basic shape for the shirt.

①

Lets draw a basic hat.

②

③

Two circles for the eyes, a triangle for the nose and a curved line for the mouth.

④ Lots of straight lines.

Lets add the details of the shirt.

⑤

⑥

We will complete the drawing with the wooden stick.

WIZARD

We will start with
a circle and a basic
shape for the shoulders.

①

Draw two
ears and an ellipse
like shape for the base
of the hat.

②

Paint the
shoulders black.

Draw a rectangle
and paint it black.

③

A star and
moon for the
earrings.

Think this shape as a wiggly triangle.

Start drawing the face and erase the extra lines.

Lets complete the face at this stage.

Draw the wand and the hand and we are done with the wizard!

WEREWOLF

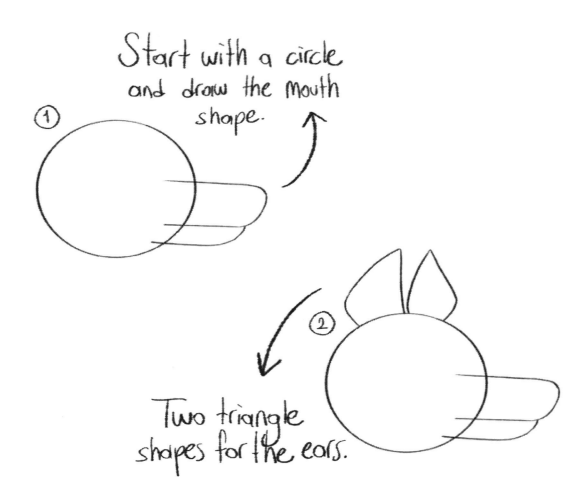

Start with a circle
and draw the mouth
shape.

①

②

Two triangle
shapes for the ears.

③

Lots of triangles for
the fur details.

Add a curved
line inside each ear.

④

Erase the
extra lines.

Don't forget his
cute teeth and nose!

⑤

Paint the nose
black.

Complete the
drawing with the remaining
details.

Suit up!

⑥

ZOMBIE

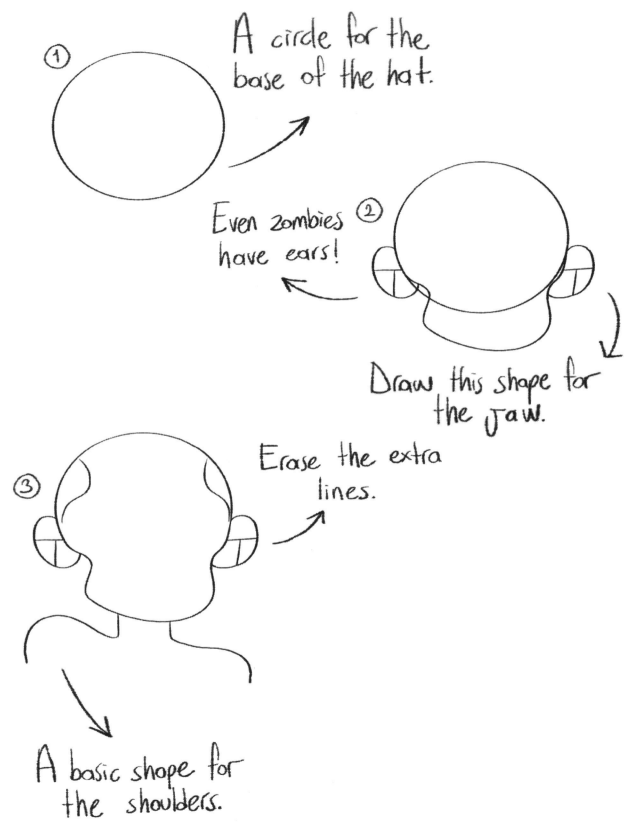

① A circle for the base of the hat.

② Even zombies have ears!

Draw this shape for the jaw.

③ Erase the extra lines.

A basic shape for the shoulders.

We will begin
with the nose and mouth.

④

Two circles for
the eyes.

⑤

Draw the eyeballs
and the teeth.

⑥

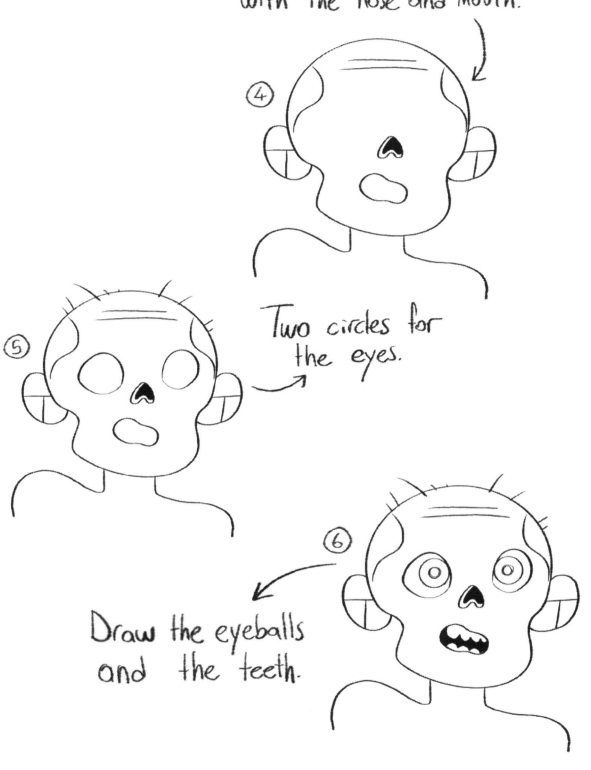

WITCH

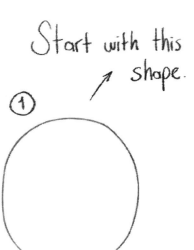

Start with this shape.

①

②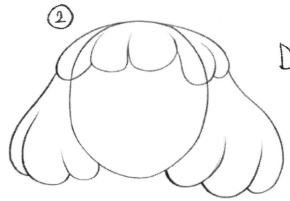

Draw these fluffy shapes for the hair.

③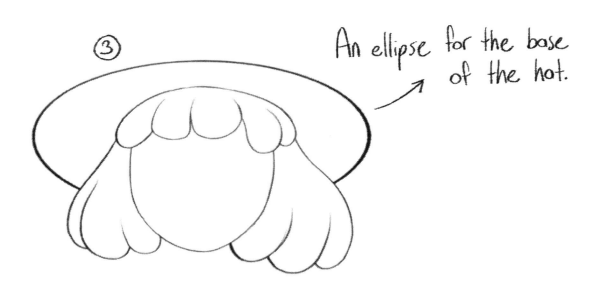

An ellipse for the base of the hat.

Add a triangle on top.

④

Draw circular shapes for the eyes.

⑤

Add the rest of the details and paint the hair!

⑥

GHOST

① Draw a circle.

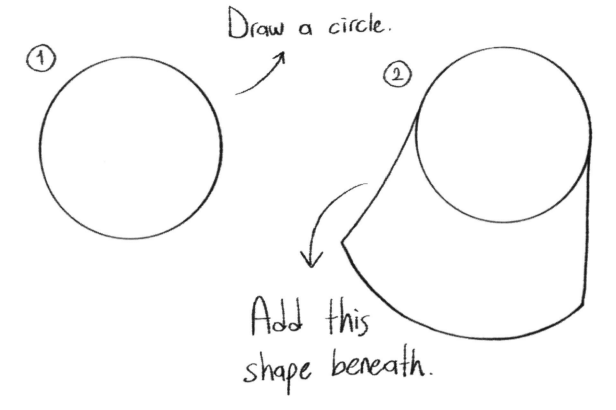

②

Add this shape beneath.

③

Repeat drawing the shapes but smaller.

④

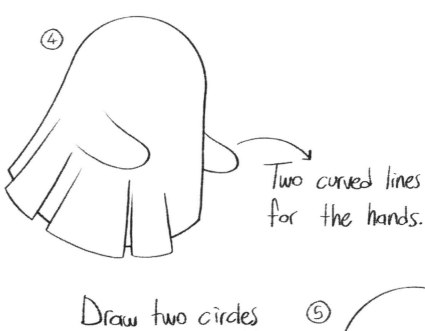

Two curved lines
for the hands.

Draw two circles
and paint them black.

⑤

Random lines for the
blush, a curved line for
the mouth and erase
two circles for the sparkles!

⑥

SKELETON

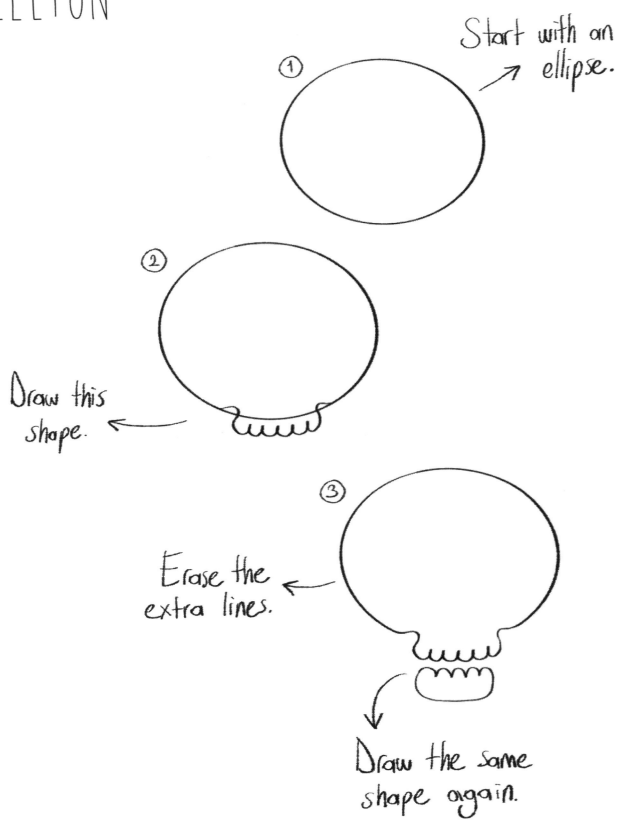

Start with an ellipse.

①

② Draw this shape.

③ Erase the extra lines.

Draw the same shape again.

④

Two circles
for the eyes.

Draw another
circle in the eyes and
paint them black.

⑤

Finish the drawing
with the rest of the
details.

⑥

WAND

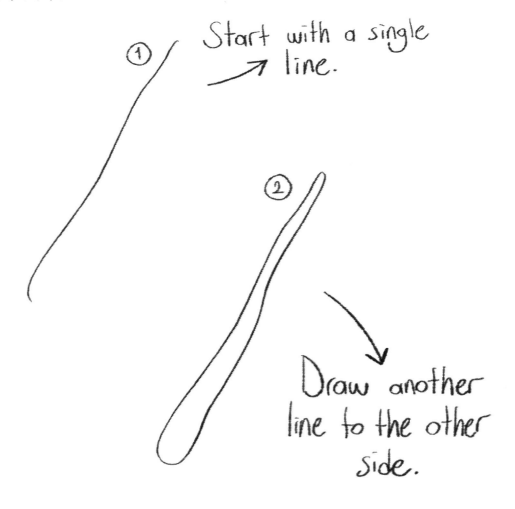

① Start with a single line.

② Draw another line to the other side.

③ A few straight lines.

Add a circle.

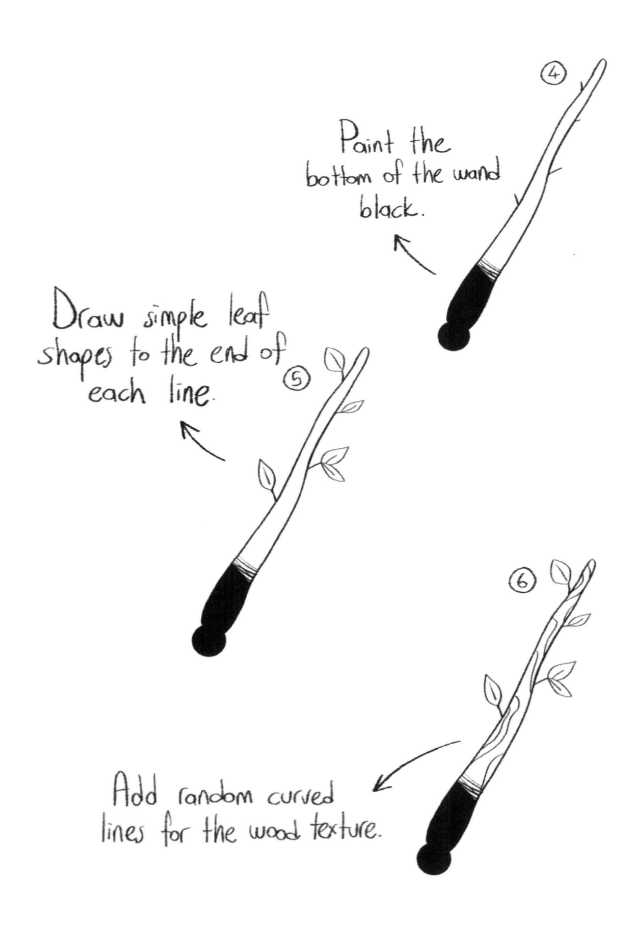

④ Paint the bottom of the wand black.

⑤ Draw simple leaf shapes to the end of each line.

⑥ Add random curved lines for the wood texture.

FULL MOON

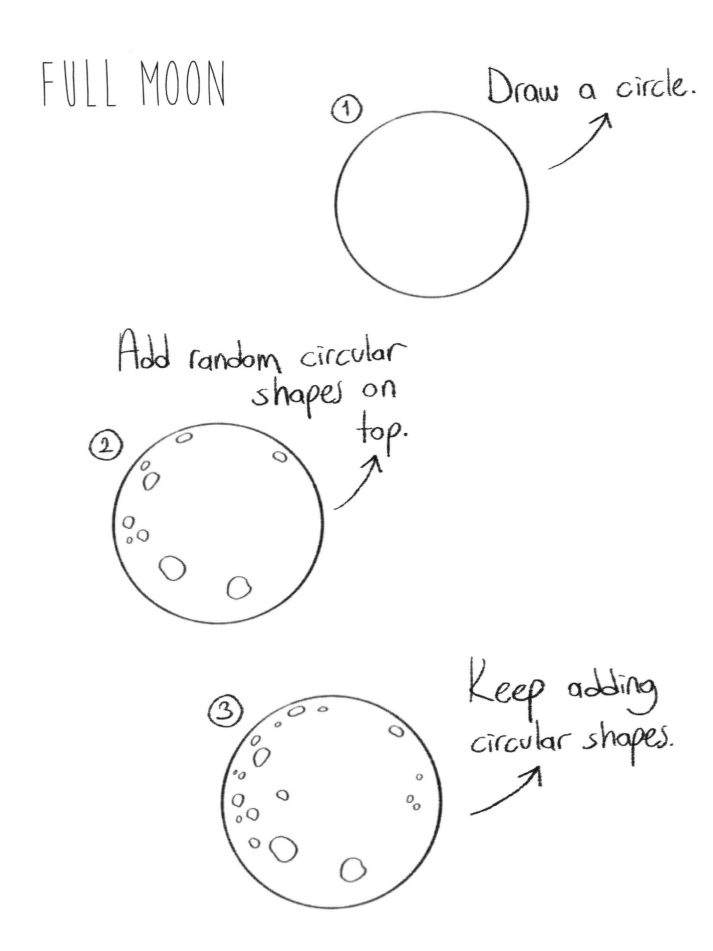

① Draw a circle.

② Add random circular shapes on top.

③ Keep adding circular shapes.

Paint the background
black.

④

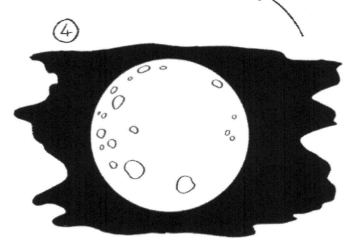

⑤

Erase some of the
areas to create
clouds.

⑥

Erase random circular
shapes for the stars and
we are done!

LANTERN

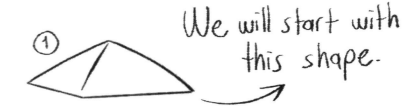

① We will start with this shape.

② Draw this black shape next.

③ Connect those two shapes with straight lines.

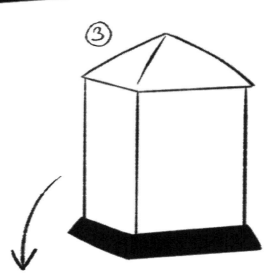

Lets add more
lines.

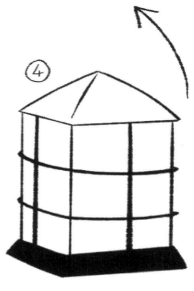

④

Draw circular lines inside
to represent the
light.

⑤

⑥

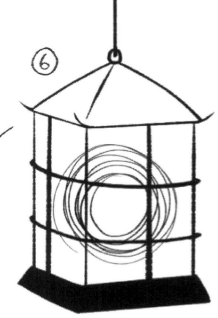

Draw one more
straight line on top!

MASK

① Draw an ellipse.

② Draw another ellipse under the first shape.

③ Add a curved line for the jaw.

Erase the extra lines.

④

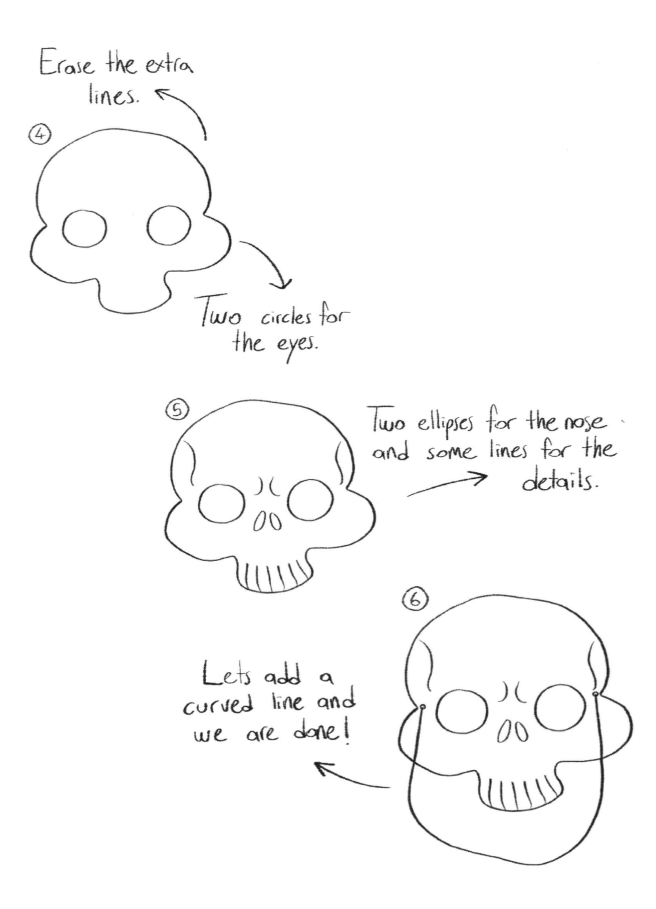

Two circles for the eyes.

⑤

Two ellipses for the nose and some lines for the details.

⑥

Lets add a curved line and we are done!

COFFIN

Lets draw the first
plane a square!

①

Draw a
rectangle.

②

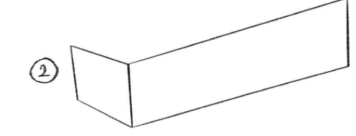

Lets add another
rectangle!

③

Keep drawing other planes.

④

Draw this shape on top.

⑤

We will finish the drawing, just draw the rest of the details.

⑥

GOBLIN

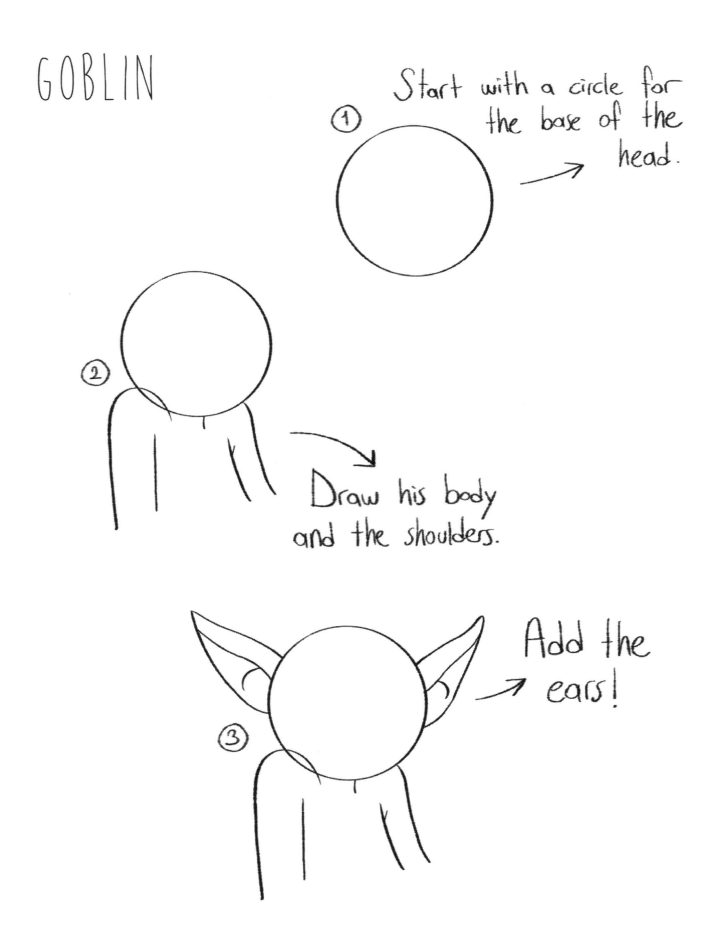

① Start with a circle for the base of the head.

② Draw his body and the shoulders.

③ Add the ears!

A fluffy hair. ④

Erase the extra lines. ⑤

Two circles for the eyes and a curved ellipse for the mouth.

A few details to here and there and we are done! ⑥

CROW

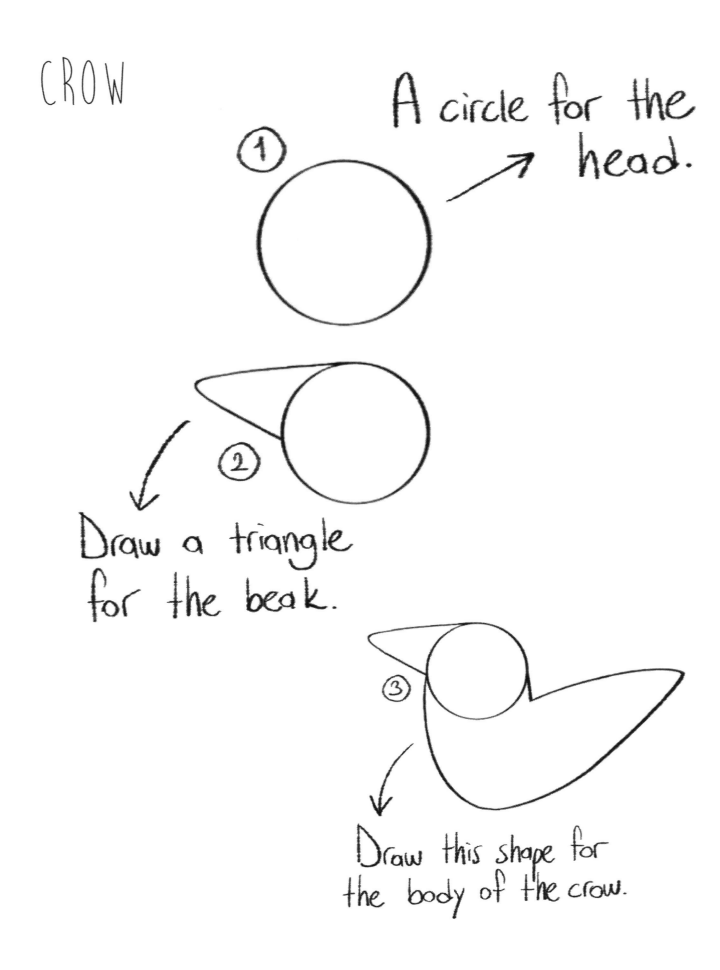

A circle for the head.

①

② Draw a triangle for the beak.

③ Draw this shape for the body of the crow.

Add these curved
lines for the fur details.

④

Paint the body black.

⑤

Some lines
for the feet of the
crow.

Erase an 'U' shape
for the eye.

⑥

SPELL BOOK

① Start with a rectangle.

② Draw this shape below.

③ Connect these two shapes.

④

Erase the extra lines. ←

Random straight lines for the page details.

Paint another rectangle on top.

⑤

Complete the drawing with the remaining details.

⑥

SPELL BOOK

GRAVESTONE

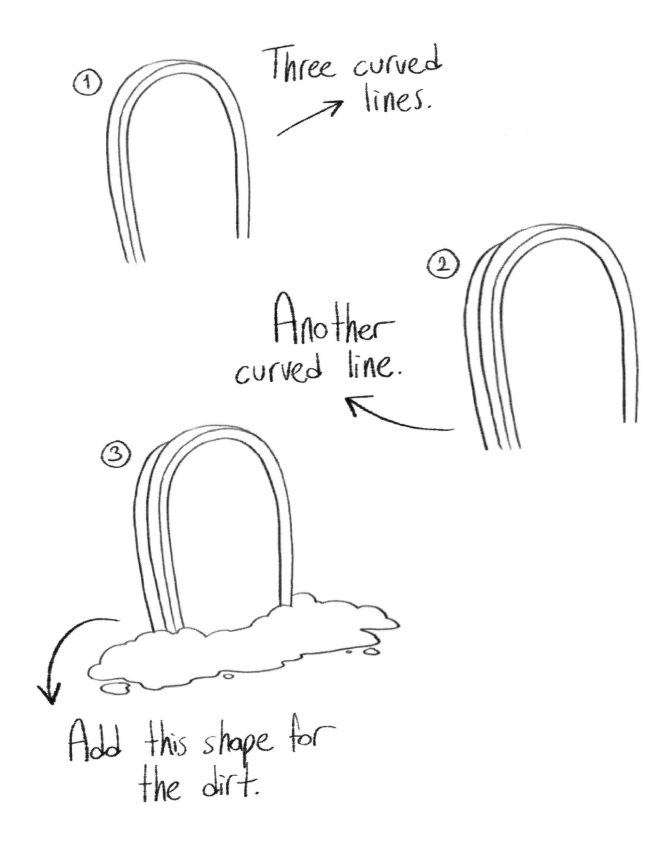

① Three curved lines.

② Another curved line.

③ Add this shape for the dirt.

Draw a black
skull.

④

Write "R.I.P."

⑤

R.I.P.

⑥

Random lines on
top of the dirt.

R.I.P.

FRANKENDOG

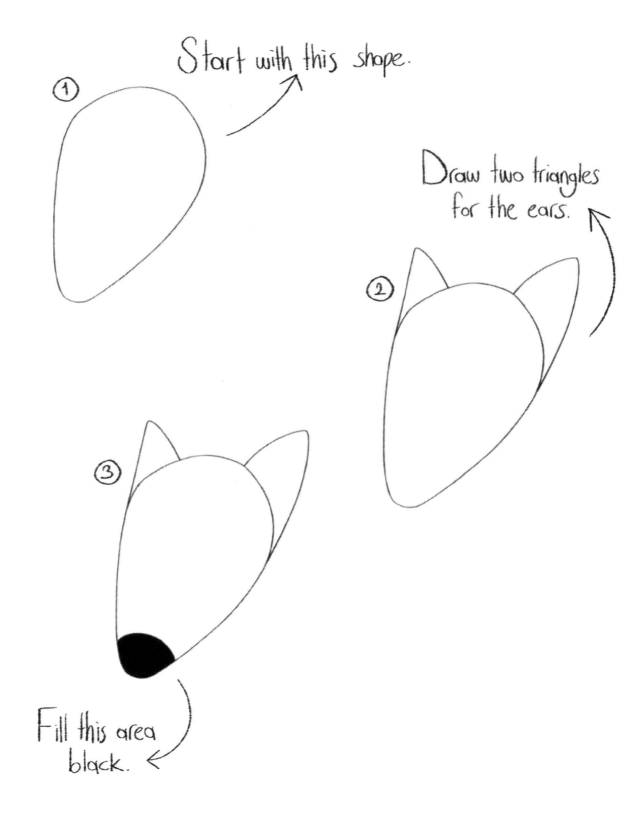

① Start with this shape.

② Draw two triangles for the ears.

③ Fill this area black.

Draw two ellipses for
the eyes and draw two more
ellipses for the eyeballs.

④

⑤

Fill these areas
black too.

Draw the remaining
details and we are done.

⑥

DEVIL

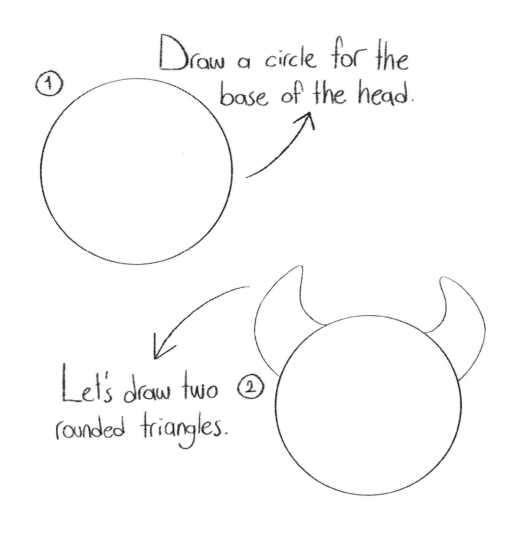

① Draw a circle for the base of the head.

② Let's draw two rounded triangles.

③ Draw two more triangles for the ears and write 'T' inside each ear.

Erase the extra lines. ④

Draw another triangle and fill it black.

Now fill the horns black.

⑤

⑥

Let's draw a face and we are done!

SPIDER

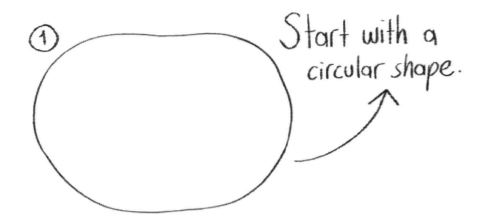

① Start with a circular shape.

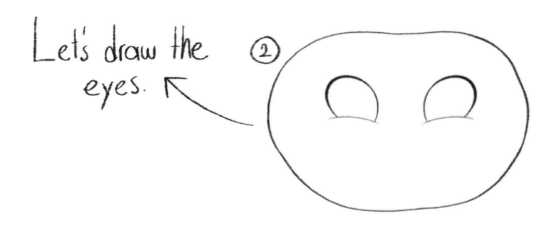

Let's draw the eyes. ②

③ Draw two circles and fill it black.

Now draw two ellipses for the blush and ④ a curved line for the mouth.

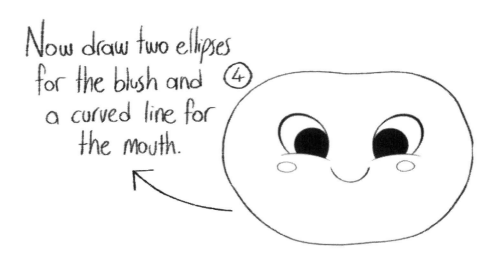

⑤

Let's start drawing a bold curved line.

Now keep drawing more bold curved lines and erase a few parts inside the eyes for the sparkle.

⑥

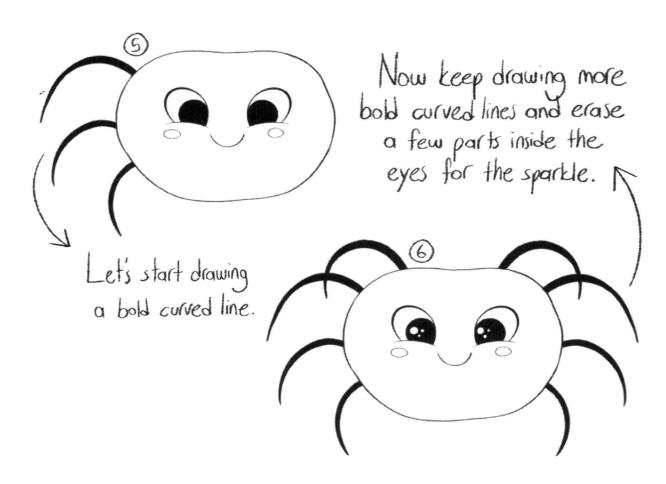

CANDY BUCKET

① Start with this shape.

② Now fill this area black.

③ Let's draw curved lines on top.

Draw triangles
for the eyes and nose.

④

⑤

Fill these areas in the
triangles black and a
bold curved line.

Now draw two
curved lines on
top.

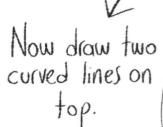 ⑥

CANDY CORN

Draw a circle.

①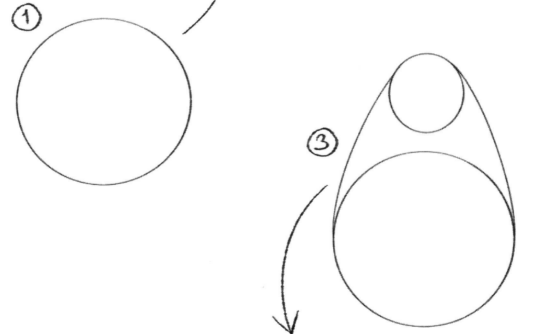

Draw a circle.

①

③

Connect the shapes with
two curved lines.

Erase the extra lines
and draw three curved lines.

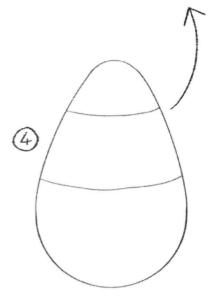
④

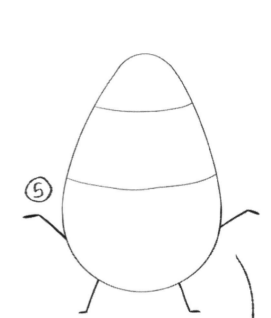
⑤

Let's draw simple lines
for the arms and legs.

Now draw a cute
face and we are done!

⑥

MUG

① Start with a rounded square.

② Now fill this area black.

③ Draw random lines here.

Draw two circles for
the eyes.

④

⑤

Fill the circles black.

Finish the drawing
with two curved lines.

⑥

BALLOON

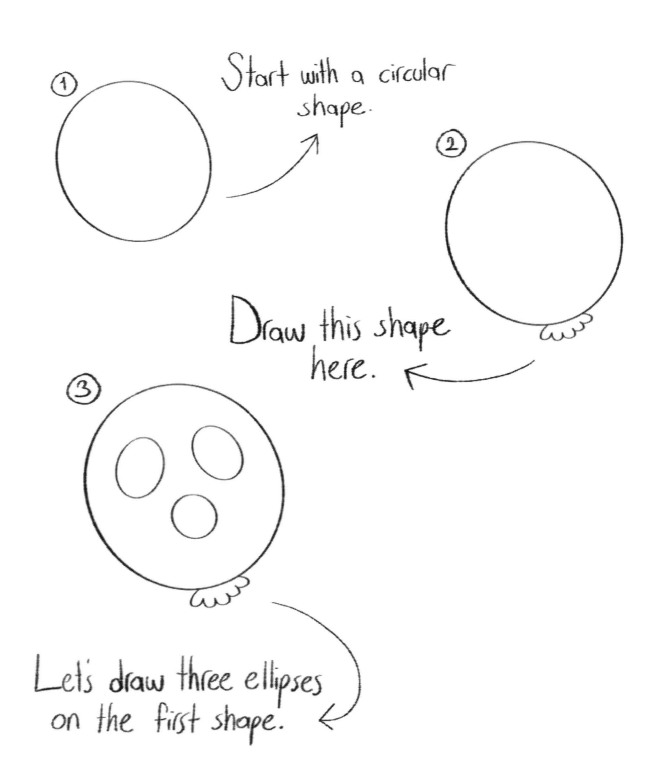

① Start with a circular shape.

② Draw this shape here. ←

③ Let's draw three ellipses on the first shape.

Fill these ellipses black. ←

④

⑤

Attach a single line.

Follow the same steps and draw the second balloon! ←

⑥

SWEATER

① Draw a basic shape for the base of the sweater.

Attach these.

②

③ Add the rectangles.

④

Draw straight lines inside the rectangles.

⑤

Fill these areas black.

Draw a skull on the sweater and we are done!

⑥

PIRATE

Start with a circle.

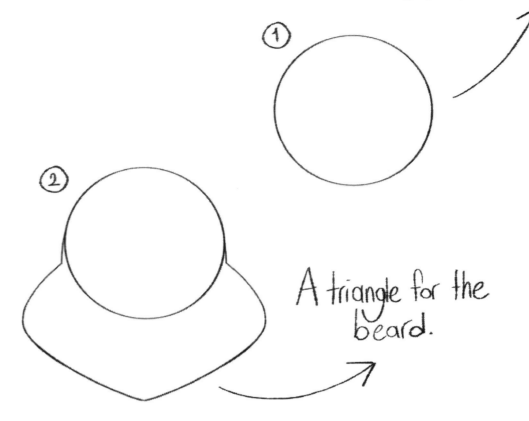

①

A triangle for the
beard.

②

Draw a curved line
and write 'T' inside for the
ears.

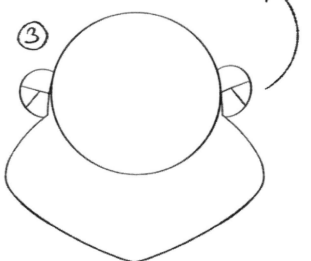

③

Let's draw the hat!

④

Draw a skull and fill it
black.

⑤

⑥

Draw a cute face
for the pirate and we
are done.

WARLOCK

Draw a circle for the
base of his head.

①

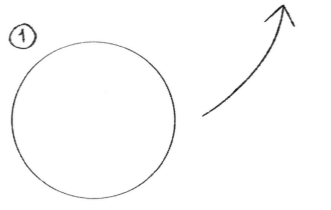

Draw lots of curved
lines for his hair.

②

Draw an ellipse for
the base of his hat.

③

Now draw a triangle.

④

Fill the hat black.

⑤

Draw a cute face and we are done!

⑥

Made in the USA
Las Vegas, NV
02 October 2021